DATE			

KEIKO's

STORY

A KILLER WHALE
GOES HOME

Linda Moore Kurth

The Millbrook Press
Brookfield, Connecticut

This book would not have happened but for the many special people who believed in Keiko, in me, and in this book: my original critique group when I was struggling to discover my direction as a writer; the staff at the Free Willy Keiko Foundation who gave me invaluable access to Keiko and his trainers; my list-serve friends who provided me with invaluable advice and support during the many troughs and crests this story encountered on its voyage to publication; my friends and relations who rallied with prayers and encouragement during the three years of this project; and to Tom, who urged me to go to Iceland and provided the resources to do so. To all of you, my deepest gratitude.

Cover photograph courtesy of Photofest.
Photographs courtesy of © Oregon Coast Aquarium: pp. 6-7 (Tim Jewett), 21 (Tim Jewett), 34 (Michael Durham), 65 (William La Marche); Photofest: p. 10; The Oregonian, Zuma: p. 14; AP/Wide World Photos: pp. 16, 17, 32, 44, 48; Steve Cowden/*The Oregonian*: pp. 19, 29, 42-43, 50, 52-53; © Shadetree Enterprises, Inc.: pp. 23, 24, 26; © Linda Moore Kurth: pp. 31 (all), 47, 58, 60; Animals Animals/Earth Scenes: p. 36 (© Johnny Johnson); The National Audubon Society Collection/Photo Researchers: pp. 38 (© 1982 F. Gohier), 40 (© 1976 Robert W. Hernandez; © Iaxelsson-Morgunbladid/ Liaison Agency: p. 59; Ocean Future's Society: p. 63

Library of Congress Cataloging-in-Publication Data
Kurth, Linda Moore.
Keiko's Story: A Killer Whale Goes Home/Linda Moore Kurth
p. cm.
Includes bibliographical references.
Summary: Describes the experiences of Keiko, the killer whale who starrred in the movie *Free Willy*, as he moved from an amusement park in Mexico to the Oregon Aquarium and then to a sea pen in Iceland, from which he may be released into the ocean.
ISBN0-7613-1500-4 (lib. bdg.)
1. Killer whale—Biography—Juvenile literature. 2. Keiko (Whale)—Juvenile lilterature. [1. Keiko (Whale) 2. Killer whale. 3. Whales.] I. Title.
QL737.C432D86 2000   599.53'6'0929—dc21   [B] 99-31963 CIP

Published by The Millbrook Press, Inc.
2 Old New Milford Road
Brookfield, Connecticut 06804
www.millbrookpress.com

R00182 09668

CONTENTS

Adiós, Amigo

"Keiko, Keiko, Keiko," the crowd shouts. "*Adiós*, Keiko. *Bien viaje*—Have a good trip.*"* It's January 7, 1996. Hundreds of families line the road to Mexico City's airport. They wave and cry and shout good-bye to the world's biggest movie star.

The people of Mexico love Keiko. It is hard to say good-bye. But they want what is best for the 7,720-pound (3,500-kg) orca. They hope that someday Keiko can be set free. They hope that maybe someday Keiko will be reunited with his family.

Keiko had been rescued from his Mexico City pool just in time. When he arrived ten years earlier, he was 10 feet (3 m) long, but over time he stretched to nearly 21 feet (6.4 m). That meant his pool was too short and too shallow for him to race and jump and dive as healthy wild orcas do. For ten years Keiko swam in chlorinated water that was thirty degrees too warm and was polluted with his own waste. For ten years he breathed the dirty air of Mexico City while starring in 7,800 performances. Every day for ten years he was hand-fed 140 pounds (64 kg) of dead fish.

Some say that Keiko was bored at Reino Aventura. His teeth were worn down from chewing on the edge of his pool. He had a virus that caused warty growths the size of extra-large pizzas

around the base of his pectoral fins. He was out of shape. A healthy whale's muscles should be tight and resilient. Pushing on Keiko was like pushing on a giant marshmallow. And although Keiko was flabby, he was at least one ton underweight. He had a droopy dorsal fin from spending so much time above water and swimming in only one direction.

Scientists think that male killer whales live on average between twenty-five and twenty-eight years in the wild—some even longer. In captivity, none have lived beyond their teens—at age nineteen, time seemed to be running out for Keiko. Doctors were especially concerned about his weakened immune system. They believed Keiko was in serious trouble.

Keiko performs at Reino Aventura in Mexico City, Mexico. See how small his pool is?

2 A Bumpy Ride to Fame

Keiko entered the world of humans when he was about two years old. In the waters of Iceland, a ship looking for young whales found him swimming with his family. Judging from other orca captures, Keiko's kidnapping might well have been traumatic. Young whales are lured into nets full of herring, then struggle to free themselves. Family members gather, circling the net and calling to their captive relatives. Not all whales survive the ordeal.

Keiko was kept at an Icelandic aquarium for two years, then sold to Marineland in Ontario, Canada, where he began his training. Being small and timid, he was harassed by the other whales. Trainers feared he lacked star quality. But Keiko was a killer whale, and killer whales, no matter how shy, fascinate people. In 1985, Reino Aventura, an amusement park near Mexico City, purchased Keiko for $350,000. There he leaped into the hearts of thousands of viewers.

FREE WILLY

While Keiko was busy entertaining the folks in Mexico City, a screenwriter by the name of Keith Walker had an inspiration.

Instead of the standard boy-and-his-dog story, he would write about a boy and his whale. It was a good, heartwarming tale about an amusement park orca named Willy. Willy's family pod finds him and calls to him from the bay outside his tank. A friendship develops between Willy and Jesse, a boy who has been separated from his own family. When Willy's greedy owner plots to kill the whale, Jesse manages to set his friend free. In the final scene, Willy is reunited with his pod.

Warner Bros. bought the *Free Willy* script and went looking for an animal to play the lead. After a massive whale hunt, producers discovered there was only one orca in the entire world that fit the role. He was the whale whom trainers once said had no star quality. He was the whale who was out of shape and underweight. He was the whale with the droopy dorsal fin. He was Keiko—about to become the world's biggest movie star.

There is something about whales that fascinates people. Perhaps it is their ancient heritage. In their present form, whales have roamed the oceans for at least ten million years and are the most intelligent life in the sea. People have gone so far as to give whales mystical qualities. Randolph, a character in the *Free Willy* movie, explained some people's view of whales: "Their eyes discovered the stars long before man was even a whisper on the Earth. They can look into a person's soul if they want." As moviegoers watched, they, too, found a connection with Willy and wanted him freed.

The makers of *Free Willy* never guessed how close to real life their story would become. Children who saw the movie became curious about its friendly black-and-white star. They learned that Keiko is the second-oldest killer whale in captivity. They discovered that Keiko's living conditions were life threatening. Like Jesse, they made up their minds to save their whale friend. Like Jesse, they hoped to reunite him with his family.

You may recognize this picture from the film "Free Willy."
Because of the movie, people found out about Keiko and
wanted to help him.

THE CHILDREN'S CAMPAIGN

Children knew there would be a price for Keiko's freedom. They began saving pennies, contributing their lunch money, organizing aluminum-can drives, and drawing pictures of Keiko to inspire others. Students at Sam Chase Elementary School in Newport, Oregon, wrote over a hundred letters asking local and national leaders to help free Keiko. President Clinton sent a letter of encouragement. Other people sent checks. That campaign netted $4,500. Said Ryan Bernardi, one of the students who helped, "It just seems right that Keiko gets the chance to be back together with his family." Schoolchildren as far apart as Tampa, Florida, and Kodiak, Alaska, organized fund-raising campaigns. Altogether, children raised nearly $100,000.

Their efforts inspired adults to lend their aid. The Earth Island Institute, an environmental and marine-mammal assistance group, got involved. Dave Phillips of Earth Island spearheaded the Free Willy Keiko campaign. He described kids as "the force behind the plan." "They put pressure on people to do the right thing," he said. The principal of Northwest Elementary School in Tampa, Florida, put it this way: "The children felt the whale was something that had a life and had rights."

Concerned scientists, including whale researcher Kenneth Balcomb, persuaded Reino Aventura to allow Keiko to be moved to a better home. Earth Island Institute stepped in and conducted a two-year search. The Institute chose the Oregon Coast Aquarium because it exists to educate people about sea life; it has an unlimited supply of good, clean seawater; it has no performing animals; and it had room to build a big new pool. The Aquarium agreed that the effort should be made to retrain Keiko so that he might be set free someday.

The Free Willy Keiko Foundation was formed in 1994 to bring Keiko to Newport and to be responsible for his rehabilitation. Warner Bros., producers of *Free Willy* and its sequels, donated $2 million to the Foundation and would later hold benefits for the Foundation. The Humane Society of the United States chipped in with $1 million. A Seattle billionaire, Craig McCaw, became Keiko's guardian angel, donating $2 million and pledging his continuing support. The greatest gift of all was Reino Aventura's donation of Keiko himself.

A home had been found for Keiko, and his pool was under construction, but moving him would be another challenge. Pat Dordan, the United Parcel Service truck driver whose route includes the Aquarium, had the answer. "Let UPS deliver Keiko," he said.

How Do You Mail a Whale?

It is January 4, 1996. Drs. Lanny Cornell and José Luis Solarzano, the veterinary team, have been practicing with Keiko for months in preparation for his move. Karla Corral and Renata Fernandez, his trainers, suspect Keiko knows he is going away. He refuses to go on for his next-to-last performance. He's not eating much.

On January 5, Keiko gives a final performance to 2,500 cheering fans. He seems to be enjoying himself as he waves a fin one last time. The crowd waves back, roaring its approval over the blasting rock music.

The big day arrives shortly after midnight. Keiko cries in high-pitched whimpers as he is hoisted out of his pool in a huge sling and suspended by a giant crane. His pectoral fins poke out of special side openings in the canvas. Karla, Renata, and the others dry Keiko with towels and rub lanolin into his skin to prevent drying. Then he is lifted high into the air. If Keiko panics, twists free, and falls, he will not survive. He squeals and waves his fins but otherwise keeps his huge body still. He is lowered into a 27-foot (8.2-m) -long waterproof fiberglass, steel, and plywood crate that will remain open at the top. It is probably the world's largest pet carrier.

Like humans, whales are warm-blooded, air-breathing mammals. Unlike us, they are voluntary breathers. That means their

Keiko is in a sling, being moved to the carrier that will hold him until he arrives in Newport, Oregon.

breathing isn't automatic; they have to think about it. While one half of their brain sleeps, the other half must stay awake. So whales can't be given sleeping pills. To lower Keiko's metabolism and keep him from overheating, his carrier is half-filled with water and 3,000 pounds (1,361 kg) of ice. The trip is calculated to take about eight and one-half hours.

As the truck bearing Keiko slowly makes its way to the airport, hundreds of people line the street saying their farewells. Delayed by the crowd, Keiko's crate is finally rolled toward the belly of the C-130 cargo plane. Thanks to Pat Dordan's suggestion, UPS has donated the use of the plane and crew. Although a little behind schedule, things are looking good. Then a roller suddenly jams and brings the loading to a screeching halt. Two frantic hours are spent repairing it while Karla and Renata try to comfort Keiko by rubbing him and murmuring assurances.

Keiko's cries hang in the air like giant question marks as his crate is finally rolled into the plane. With him are his doctors, who will monitor his body functions during the 3,000-mile (4,828-km) trip. Keiko has not been fed for twenty-four hours. No airline snacks will be waiting for him, either. No one wants an airsick whale on their hands.

Karla and Renata follow Keiko in a chase jet. They will spend the next several months in Newport, helping him adjust.

The plane lands in Phoenix, Arizona, to refuel. All of the ice in Keiko's carrier has melted, and the water is too warm. His doctors worry that he could become overheated and die. Although it means another nerve-racking delay, they order 2,000 more pounds (907 kg) of ice and a change of water for his crate. Karla and Renata continue to reassure him.

In the meantime, workers in Newport are making doubly sure Keiko's pool is ready. They check the water temperature, salinity (saltiness), and filtration systems. They have been working day and night preparing for Keiko's arrival. They are proud and excited.

After eighteen and one-half long hours, Keiko's plane arrives in Newport. A paradelike caravan rolls toward the Oregon Coast Aquarium. The children and their parents have been waiting in the rain to see their favorite whale. They hold up soggy home-made banners. "WELCOME TO OREGON, KEIKO!" and "YEA, KEIKO!" Ron Kay drives the UPS truck carrying Keiko and his crate. Recognizing his droopy dorsal fin rising above the crate, the crowd breaks into cheers. Keiko responds with his own squeals and a couple of misty puffs of air. There is a police escort. Pat Dordan waves from his delivery van. Finally they reach their destination. Phyllis Bell, president of the Aquarium, signs the delivery form. She's just accepted the largest and liveliest package the Aquarium has ever seen.

Fans of the famous killer whale didn't mind the rain as they stood along the streets to greet Keiko.

Fans in England, Finland, Australia, and across the United States have been watching Keiko's journey on TV. They hold their breath, hoping Keiko will be okay. They hope Keiko will like his new home.

A big yellow crane hooks onto Keiko's sling. It swings the whale over the high walls of his tank. After hours of being a good whale, Keiko is ready for freedom. Perhaps it is the smell of salt water that beckons him. As he is lowered toward the water, he begins thrashing his tail and squealing with impatience. His sling is eased into the water. Keepers in wet suits scramble to clear the cables out of Keiko's way. Keiko pushes free and takes a deep dive. Slowly he begins swimming, exploring his new quarters. Karla and Renata are there, waiting for him. They are familiar faces in unfamiliar surroundings. "*Hola, amigo,*" they say as they feed him his first meal after the long trip. Everyone breathes a sigh of relief. Watchers whoop and clap. Reporters send news to London and Tokyo. The world rejoices that Keiko is one step closer to freedom.

Karla and Renata feed Keiko after his journey from Mexico City, Mexico, to Newport, Oregon.

KEIKO'S OREGON HOME

COST: $7.3 MILLION

150 FEET (45 M) LONG,
ABOUT HALF THE LENGTH OF A FOOTBALL FIELD

25 FEET (7.6 M) DEEP

75 FEET (22.8 M) WIDE

VOLUME: 2 MILLION GALLONS (7.5 MILLION L)

CHANGEABLE WATER CURRENT—CLOCKWISE,
COUNTERCLOCKWISE,
SCRAMBLED—TO DISCOURAGE
SINGLE-DIRECTION SWIMMING

ROCKY REEF JUTTING AS HIGH AS TEN FEET

PLAY JETS CAPABLE OF SENDING UP A CURTAIN
OF WATER OR MANY BUBBLES

RUBBING ROCKS

MEDICAL POOL—FOR EXAMINATIONS
33 FEET (10 M) LONG
28 FEET (8.5 M) WIDE
9 (2.7 M) FEET DEEP

VIEWERS GALLERY

TRAINERS' ROOM

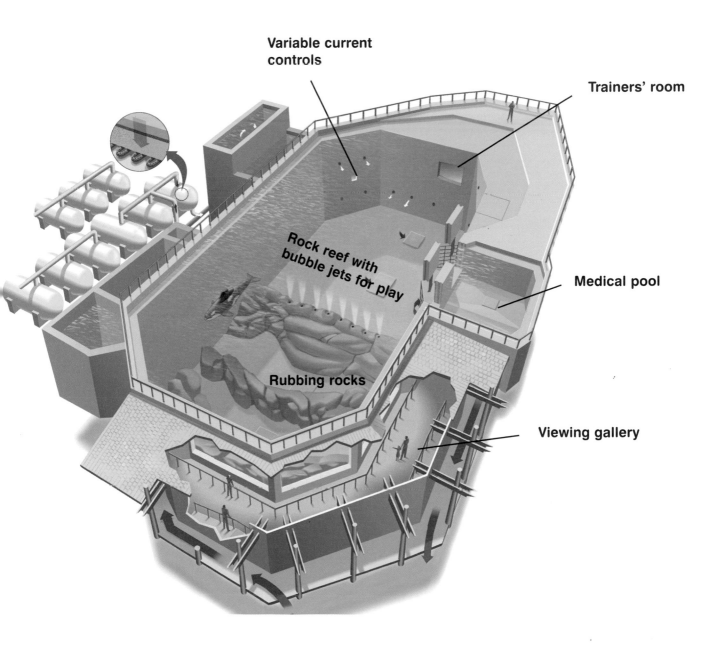

Variable current controls

Trainers' room

Rock reef with bubble jets for play

Rubbing rocks

Medical pool

Viewing gallery

4 Getting to Know Keiko

Life with Keiko was exciting for Karla Corral and Renata Fernandez. Karla worked with Keiko for five years in Mexico City, where she also trained dolphins and seals. She got in the habit of telling Keiko her problems. Karla said he was a good listener. "He's very loving. He talks to me in his way. I think he is even smarter than we are."

After four years of working with Keiko, Renata saw his humanlike qualities, too. Keiko had been known to abandon his act and leave for an adjacent pool when he'd missed a trick. Could he have been mad at himself? Renata described Keiko as being like "a little kid" sometimes, but also "noble and kind." He seemed attuned to their moods. When one of them didn't feel like working hard, Keiko didn't want to work, either.

Renata and Karla often rode on Keiko's back during performances. The women became celebrities when they were filmed for a Mexico TV miniseries featuring their work with the famous orca. They stayed with Keiko at the Oregon Coast Aquarium for six months until he felt secure with his new staff. Upon leaving, Karla was in tears. "Keiko is my best friend," she said. "I know I am leaving the most important part of my life behind."

Karla (in this picture) and Renata rode on Keiko in many performances in Mexico City.

Killer Facts

Dental abscesses are one of the main causes of death in wild whales.

Killer Facts

Scientists believe that whales evolved from four-footed creatures. Whale skeletons reveal small pelvic bones, which are the remnants of hind legs. Many fossils have been discovered, reflecting the full transition from four-legged land animal, to an aquatic form with reduced (but present) hind limbs, to oceanic forms with no external hind appendages.

At the Aquarium, ten full-time marine mammalogists were permanently assigned to Keiko. They often came in after hours to check on him and to keep him company. During exercise breaks, Keiko seemed to enjoy them lounging on his back while they tried to catch a bit of rare Oregon sun. Those moments recalled Native American tales of people walking on the backs of wild orcas to prove their bravery.

PARTY TIME

Orcas are social animals with strong family bonds. In Mexico City, the park often threw parties where up to thirty people swam with Keiko. Two bottlenose dolphins also shared his pool. Although Keiko's new pool was just the right temperature for him, it was too cold for the dolphins. Since the Foundation couldn't find him a marine mammal companion, his trainers had to act as his family pod.

Orca skin is thin and sensitive to touch. Orcas often rub their bodies on one another. Sometimes they even rake their teeth over one another. Keiko clearly enjoyed having his back and fins stroked and scratched. When his trainers rubbed his belly, his tail quivered like a dog's back leg. Keiko gave his human playmates gentle shoves across the pool. He'd dive under a trainer, then bomb out of the water with a human playmate on his nose for a wild "rocket ride." He'd entice his trainers to stand on his back or his cheek, then shake them off. He'd open his mouth and curl his tongue at them. Keiko's tongue is about the size and texture of a rough bath mat. They'd reach beyond his vicious-looking teeth and scratch it.

There is always an element of danger in working with such a large animal. In 1991, a trainer was accidentally drowned while playing alone with three orcas. The rule at the Aquarium was never to be in the pool with Keiko without another trainer nearby.

TOTE THAT PAIL

Taking care of Keiko at the Aquarium wasn't all fun and games. It was smelly and messy, too. Fish-house duty started at 6:30 in the morning. Keiko often cruised over to the trainers' window to say good morning and to watch their activities. Trainers had to defrost hundreds of pounds of fish, not just for Keiko but for the Aquarium's otters, seals, and sea lions. Keiko's freezer held up to a year's supply of food—120,000 pounds (54,431 kg) of frozen fish. That's as much as all the other animals at the aquarium eat combined. Hauling the fish in buckets to Keiko and his fellow Aquarium residents took strong muscles.

Who would have thought that being a whale-keeper meant you'd have to be a janitor, too? Vacuuming Keiko's pool—

Killer Facts

Killer whales and other toothed whales are not really whales at all. They are members of the dolphin family.

Keiko gets his fin rubbed by an Oregon trainer. Keiko likes to be touched by the people he works with.

Always curious, Keiko takes a look as his pool in Newport, Oregon, is cleaned. The divers are used to the attention.

a one-hour job—was on every trainer's work schedule. Not so bad, though, when you think of what elephant trainers have to deal with!

REGULAR CHECKUPS

Whales may not appear ill until their condition is critical. Trainers checked on Keiko's health daily. They smelled his breath as he released it through his blowhole. Bad breath often means a whale is sick. They asked Keiko to open his mouth so they could check his gums and teeth. Just as you might feel a dog's ears for signs of a fever, they felt Keiko's tail for hot spots, a sign of infection.

More complicated tests were sometimes needed. In Newport, a small, shallow medical pool was attached to the big pool. It allowed Keiko's doctors to draw blood from his tail, extract his stomach contents through a tube inserted down his throat, and apply suction cups to his body so they could measure his cardiovascular capacity. Trainers had to teach Keiko to cooperate with the doctors. He learned to float belly-up during blood sampling. Since a whale's "nostril" is on top of his head, it was a good time to test how long Keiko could hold his breath.

Killer Facts

Although adult male and female dorsal fins are quite different, it's hard to tell the difference between the dorsal fins of young males and those of mature females. Curled dorsal fins are common among 5 to 10 percent of wild whales and do not negatively affect their swimming.

Killer Facts

Killer whales can dive as deep as 1,000 feet (305 m) because of the marine mammal diving response. Their lungs collapse during the dive. When the whales return to the surface, their lungs expand.

Killer Facts

When seeing an orca, some gray whales are known to go into shock and lie on their back, waiting to die.

Keiko is having blood taken so it can be tested. He learned to hold his breath and float upside down for his trainers.

Killer Facts

Scientists can tell the approximate age of whales by examining the rings of their teeth—similar to studying the rings of trees.

JUST KIDDING!

Keiko may be a friendly animal, but that doesn't mean that every acquaintance is automatically his pal. Keiko often tested his new trainers. More than once, he'd hold a trainer's leg in his mouth. It took lots of scratching, rubbing, and soothing words to convince the killer whale to let go.

As Keiko's health improved, so did his sense of humor and growing independence. Brian O'Neal, one of Keiko's trainers, described how Keiko teased him. If Brian asked Keiko to do a bow-breach, the whale might do a barrel roll instead. If Brian next asked Keiko to do a barrel roll, he'd do a bow-breach. Sometimes, upon receiving a command, Keiko would shake his head side-to-side and squeal, as if to say, "I'm not gonna!"

"He's a goof," said Nolan Harvey, Keiko's longtime trainer.

Killer Facts

Adult male orcas are, on average, as long as a school bus. That's about 32 feet (9.7 m).

Female orcas are about 27 feet (8.2 m) in length.

5 Training Camp

No wonder Keiko seemed excited upon entering his Newport pool. For the first time in years, he had room to dive and spyhop (see page 43) in cold, clean seawater.

The reeflike rockwork on the floor of Keiko's tank was a much more natural setting than the standard swimming pools that Keiko had lived in before. There were crags and canyons to explore and rocks to rub against. In the wild, orcas seek out special rocky beaches to rub off loose skin. Within six months of his arrival, Keiko was able to rub off an entire layer of old skin.

The whale-size canyons in the reef provided interesting opportunities for Keiko to practice his echolocation, a natural sonar that whales use to locate objects. Whales send out high-pitched sounds that travel through the water, bounce off the object, and travel back to them in a kind of sound picture. The picture shows the size, density, and shape of the object. Since sound travels five times faster in water than in air, it's a quick way to determine what's out there.

WATER AEROBICS

"You're the whale!" "Super dude!" "Woo who, Keiko!" Keiko's trainers shouted and clapped encouragement as they put the whale through his paces. They urged him to do more swimming underwater, to exercise longer, farther, and quicker than the time before.

Though Keiko was no longer performing, the Aquarium was more like a training camp than a retirement home. In the wild, orcas often swim 50 to 100 miles (80–160 km) a day. An important step toward freedom was to build up Keiko's strength and stamina. Several times a day his trainers coached him in aerobic workouts. They used voice commands, hand motions, and a high-pitched whistle called a bridge to guide him. Behaviors included fast swims underwater, breaching, barrel rolls, and backward leaps.

In Mexico City, Keiko often lounged at the edge of the pool. The warm water made him lazy—a real "pool potato." When Keiko arrived in Newport, he was lazy, but he was also smart. In fact, it took trainers the entire first week at the Aquarium to figure out he was cheating. Instead of doing laps at top speed, Keiko would swim down to the end of his pool, wait for the wave he'd just made, and surf back on it. A year later, Keiko was

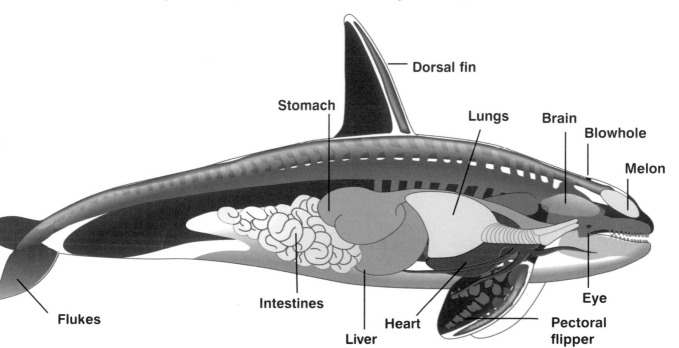

Dorsal fin

Stomach

Lungs Brain

Blowhole

Melon

Intestines

Heart

Eye

Flukes

Liver

Pectoral flipper

Killer Sonar

Killer whales use their special brand of sonar called *echolocation* by bouncing high-pitched sounds off objects and receiving the resulting echoes. Echolocation helps in hunting and navigation.

Making the sound

Air passages located below the blowhole produce clicks. The thick oil in the melon (see diagram on page 29) directs the clicks toward the object the whale wants to "see."

Receiving the sound

Although whales have tiny external ears, scientists doubt that they are functional. Sound waves are picked up in the animal's lower jaw. They are then directed to the inner ear via fat within the lower jaw. In this way, whales can locate objects and tell their distance, size, and shape in a kind of "sound picture."

making up his own vigorous workouts, breaching and speed-swimming on his own.

To encourage Keiko to develop independent, creative thinking, trainers rewarded him for inventing his own exercises. Keiko was given a signal, which meant "Make something up." Having been told exactly what to do for eighteen years, Keiko was puzzled and frustrated by these new commands. After lots of practice by Keiko and tons of patience from his trainers, he began to catch on. At one session, Keiko came up with forty different behaviors. He invented "moon walking" on the bottom of the pool and squirting water out of his mouth at low-passing gulls, backward spyhopping, and bouncing backward on his tail. Keiko taught himself to swim upside down, to move his tongue against the water current, and to shake his pectoral fins. As he began feeling better, Keiko jazzed up these behaviors even further—doing an extra barrel roll or squirting water through his teeth while performing a breach—as if to give his trainers a little extra something to think about.

HERRING FROM HEAVEN

Because frozen fish lose some nutritional benefits, Keiko was given a daily dose

At the Oregon Coast Aquarium, Keiko was asked to be creative, so he invented all sorts of new tricks.

of forty sea-tabs, marine-mammal multivitamins. They were about the size of human vitamins and fortified with kelp. Keiko's mother didn't teach him to chew his food; orcas swallow their fish whole. Keiko swallowed 50 pounds (23 kg) of fish a day without having to do any tricks.

Feeding times and amounts varied during the day—part of his "surprise" conditioning. For eighteen years, Keiko's food had come in a bucket, and it had always been dead fish. At the Aquarium, Keiko ate a total of 185 pounds (84 kg) of herring, capelin, and squid every day. At nine 20-pound buckets, he consumed as much food as the other animals in the Aquarium combined. To get Keiko used to feeling a live, wiggling fish in his mouth, trainers stunned the fish before feeding him. Little by

Keiko is fed a bucket of squid by Peter Noah, one of his trainers in Oregon.

little they stunned the fish less and less until Keiko learned to eat them.

Whales have been called desert dwellers because they drink so little water—only about a gallon (3.8 l) of seawater a day. The rest of their water comes from their food. Squid have a high water content, but they've been an acquired taste for Keiko. The first time he was fed one of the slippery critters, he promptly spit it out.

Keiko's trainers worked long and hard to teach him to catch the live fish in his tank. At first he was a catch-and-release fisherman, rolling a fish around in his mouth, then letting it go. A real breakthrough came one night when an Aquarium security guard heard Keiko vocalizing and swimming about in his medical pool. The next morning his trainers found the partially eaten remains of a black cod at the bottom of the pool. It was probably the first time Keiko had caught and eaten a fish without being told do so. By the time Keiko left for Iceland, about half his diet was the live fish he'd caught himself.

HOW DO YOU WEIGH A WHALE?

Keiko was coaxed into a sling, and a crane with a digital scale hoisted him up and recorded his weight. In June 1997, he weighed in at 9,620 pounds (4,364 kg). That's the gain that Dr. Cornell had hoped for. Most of Keiko's weight was muscle. Pushing on Keiko's side had become like pushing against a firm, wet soccer ball.

Between weigh-ins, Keiko was measured regularly with a tape. He'd hold it in his mouth while his caretakers stretched it along his massive body to the tip of his tail. Measurements were also taken around Keiko's middle.

With all the exercise, good food, and cold, clean water at the Aquarium, Keiko's skin virus disappeared. Doctors said this was a sign that his immune system had been shaping up, too.

People of all ages are fascinated by Keiko and helped to get him back to Iceland.

As well as being much bigger, Keiko's most visible change was to his dorsal fin. Because Keiko's back muscles had been strengthened, the top of the fin's curl was about 12 inches (30.5 cm) higher.

BRAIN GAMES

Mental exercises are as important as the physical ones. At first, Keiko was interested in a big-screen TV installed for him. Saturday night wrestling was a favorite. But the novelty soon wore off, and the TV was removed. Keiko showed much interest in a small toy orca and a pet rat, both of which were placed on a shelf in front of the keepers' viewing window.

Having been a working whale most of his life, Keiko had to be taught to play. One at a time, trainers introduced Keiko to a new toy by encouraging him to touch it with the top of his head, his pectoral fins, and other parts of his body. Then they'd show him how to push the toy, tow it, or otherwise manipulate it. After some work, he got the hang of it and enjoyed pushing a heavy blue rubber ball around with his nose. Another toy was a large inner tube that he often gently grasped with his teeth. Sometimes he'd take one of his toys to the bottom of his pool, then let it shoot to the surface.

Most encouraging of all was Keiko's attitude. He worked hard at the Aquarium.

A Whale of a Question

Can Keiko adapt to being a wild orca once again? Dr. Cornell thinks so. After all, the doctor reasons, small dolphins have been successfully released to the wild. Orcas are simply the largest members of the dolphin family. A pilot whale named Bimbo was returned to his native waters off California after being in captivity for eight years. Two years later he was sighted swimming with other wild pilot whales. J. J., a gray whale calf found stranded as an infant, was nursed back to health and released in the vicinity of migrating gray whales in 1998. J. J. scraped off her tracking device, so no one knows how she is.

Some experts have said that Keiko is too nice, not aggressive enough to cope with the rigors of the sea. Ann D. Terbush, M.D., is chief of the Permits Division for the National Marine Fisheries Service. She referred to an unsuccessful release of nine captive dolphins in 1992 and warned that reality is often more cruel than we'd like to think.

ORCINUS ORCA

To help determine if and when Keiko is ready, orca behavior must be understood. Killer whales are the most widely distributed marine mammal in the world. The scientific name for killer whales is *Orcinus orca*—*orcinus* meaning "of or belonging to

A male, with the tall dorsal fin, and a female orca swim in Glacier Bay, in Glacier Bay National Park, Alaska. The mountains in the background are part of the Fairweather Range.

the realm of the dead" and *orca*, "a kind of whale." Killer whales got their common name from mistranslating the Spanish word that means "whale killers." With their striking black-and-white coloring and their playful spirit, killer whales are the splashiest stars of the sea. They are also the oceans' greatest predators.

Except for a few cases of mistaken identification, there is no evidence that killer whales have any interest in attacking people. A recent event in Japan demonstrated the orca's gentle behavior toward humans. At that time, Japanese fishermen captured ten orcas to be sold to aquariums. While the orca mothers were extremely distressed at being separated from their babies, not once did any of them attack the fishermen.

Orcas are part of an order of marine mammals called Cetacea. Like all mammals, they are warm-blooded, breathe with their lungs, give live birth, and are nourished by their mother's milk.

The size and shape of the animal's dorsal fin and the shape of the gray area behind the fin, called a saddle patch, can identify individuals. Male orcas may have a dorsal fin that is as tall as 6 feet (1.8 m) and often has nicks and scars on it. Females are smaller than males and have shorter, curved dorsal fins. Researchers study hundreds of photographs of whales to help them gauge the health of the pods as well as their habits.

ORCA SOCIETY

Members of the pod communicate with one another through squeaks, whistles, and shrill calls as well as echolocation. Calves learn how to vocalize from their mothers and other members of the pod. Each calf has a distinct voice.

There are perhaps 10,000 orcas in the world today. They inhabit all the oceans of the world, preferring the Arctic, the Antarctic, and other cold waters. Many orcas have been slaughtered or captured because fishermen see them as competition for fish. But orcas are not considered to be as tasty as other whales, nor do they yield as much fatty oil, so they have not been hunted to the extent of other whales. An adult orca has no enemies other than humans.

The most intensive studies of orcas have been in the Pacific Northwest. Two distinct societies of orcas have been identified, the **resident** and the **transient**. The social structure of each society is organized around its food source.

RESIDENTS

The diet of the resident community in the Pacific Northwest consists of fish—mostly salmon—and squid. Resident whale groups usually stay at least six months in their own general area or range, not far from shore.

The social structure of resident orcas revolves around a **matrilineal group,** consisting of a mother and her children and her daughters' offspring. They always travel and rest together. Up to five subpods often travel together in a **pod** of ten to twenty individuals that are all related to one another. It is not known how an orca family regroups when the head orca mother dies.

Young whales nurse for about two years, then their rearing is often taken over by female relatives of the mother or "aunties." Occasionally a juvenile male cousin will become a temporary baby-sitter. Even as adults, the males do not stray far from their mothers. Neither do they seem to fight with one another for dominance as many other wild male animals do. Mating occurs when pods meet and mingle, usually in the spring.

Orcas swim along the shore in Washington State.

The family bond among orcas is remarkably strong. If one member is stranded on a beach or captured, the family usually refuses to abandon that member even though their own lives may be in peril. Orcas have been seen helping injured or ill members of the pod to swim and breathe. The pod hunts together, too, often rounding up its prey before attacking. No wonder orcas have been nicknamed "wolves of the sea."

Although there is much coordinated activity, researchers don't know just how decisions are made. Observers think that pod members communicate about where to go and what to do. They call to one another when separated and when hunting. Each resident pod has between five and fifteen different calls.

Pods sometimes join together into a large **clan** or **super pod**. The clan shares a **dialect,** or common method of communication. Scientists have little knowledge about the meaning of this speech. Whale watchers have described the joining of pods as a reunion party with much vocalization, chasing, leaping, lobtailing, and fin slaps. Often there is mating between the pods. After traveling together for a time, the whales eventually return to their original pods.

TRANSIENTS

Transient orcas may travel alone or in groups of up to seven individuals. A group might be made up of a mother and one or two offspring or a small group of females. They have no specific territory and roam over a large area of the ocean. They stay under water longer than resident orcas and have fewer calls than residents do. Perhaps this is because they sneak up on their prey— other marine animals such as seals, sea lions, porpoises, penguins, whales, and even the largest animal on earth, the blue whale.

The hunting behavior of transients can be cunning. When encountering prey on small ice floes, the transients are known to swim under the ice, tipping it with their backs and dumping their next meal into the sea. Or they may barrel their huge bodies

A killer whale takes a close look at a seal meal. Moments after this photo was taken, the seal dove into the water and was eaten.

onto the ice, frightening their prey into the icy waters.

Another group called the **offshore** whales is largely a mystery. It is much harder to study these orcas because they range far out to sea and are rarely seen.

NORTH ATLANTIC ORCAS

North Atlantic orcas number about 6,000 animals. They migrate from Iceland's Westman Islands, up Iceland's east coast and over to Norway, a jaunt of more than 1,000 miles (1,600 km). Gisli Vikingsson of Iceland's Marine Research Institute says that in the two years he had observed orcas in the Westman Islands their family patterns appeared to be similar to the Pacific Northwest orcas. Researchers are guessing that the North Atlantic orcas may also be made up of residents and transients, since some groups chase the herring and other groups hunt marine mammals.

The fish-eating orcas work together to corral small herring into tight balls underwater. As the group circles the fish, individual orcas take turns dashing to the center and scooping up a mouthful. Keiko was caught with a group of orcas chasing the herring. He will need to form an association with a pod of resident orcas if he is to take part in cooperative hunting.

Even in the Pacific Northwest, researchers do not know what happens to orcas that find themselves permanently separated from their mother's pod.

Lessons 7 From Keiko

One typically cloudy day at the Aquarium, Dr. Cornell came to see his most famous patient. After the routine checkup, Dr. Cornell began whistling to Keiko the way Renata and Karla once had. Keiko suddenly began a series of killer-whale vocalizations. It was as if an early memory had been triggered, releasing a flood of sounds.

Keiko's new sounds had a profound effect on the people responsible for him. Until then, the Free Willy Keiko Foundation had been largely concerned with bringing Keiko back to health. Now that he was speaking a "language" possibly learned in childhood, they realized they had only begun to consider what it meant to free Keiko and needed to study his vocalizations.

RECORDING ROUND THE CLOCK

A first step was to record Keiko's speech with four underwater microphones called hydrophones. Scientists from Woods Hole Oceanographic Institution recorded his vocalizations twenty-four hours a day. At the same time, cameras above and below water filmed his actions. Researchers hope this will help them to link orca sounds to orca behavior. They also gathered recordings made by scientists in Iceland, Norway, and other parts of

Breaching

Leaping clear out of the water and landing on the back or side in a breach may be an orca's way of startling prey. It may also be a way of showing off or just having a whale of a good time. Orcas have been seen performing synchronized breaching as pods greet each other.

Lobtailing

Orcas can use their powerful tail flukes as a club to knock out seals and sea lions. They may also swing their tail, or flukes, in a lobtail if they are angry.

the Atlantic, creating the first comprehensive library of North Atlantic killer-whale vocalizations.

Keepers have gotten Keiko accustomed to wearing a heart-rate monitor, attached by a suction cup. It was sometimes used in the Aquarium pool, on his trip to Iceland, and then in the sea pen. They also attached a tiny video camera dubbed the "Keiko Cam" near his forehead. It can record what Keiko sees under-water. Other devices can record the depth and time of Keiko's dives and his swimming speed. All this activity makes Keiko the most studied marine mammal in the world.

Moves

Slapping

Orcas sometimes slap their pectoral fins to herd fish or stun and kill small marine mammals. It may also be a way of communicating with other orcas.

Spyhopping

When orcas want to see what's going on above the water, they spyhop. It looks like a tail-stand with the head above water. Spyhopping allows orcas to see other whales or boats or, if they're the sort that eat marine mammals, to locate their next seal meal.

THE CONTROVERSY

Some people question the wisdom of spending millions of dollars on a single animal like Keiko. They think the money could be better used fighting world hunger, solving pollution problems, or saving the rain forests.

Keiko's supporters take another view. Naomi Rose of the U.S. Humane Society wrote, "What we learn from Keiko and others could help save an endangered species someday and also teach us so much more about orcas and their family bonds, their memories, and their intelligence."

Keiko is always interested in what goes on around him and who's looking at him, just like these children are.

If Keiko is successfully released, he will be the first orca to be returned to the wild after an extended time in captivity. Other orcas now in captivity might benefit from Keiko's experience. Lolita in Miami and Corky in San Diego are excellent candidates for release, since their pods have been identified. Corky has the best chance of returning because her mother is still alive. But orca shows bring in large profits to marine parks. The owners of Lolita and Corky view their orcas as valuable property. Despite pleas from various groups, neither Lolita nor Corky has yet been able to follow Keiko's path to freedom.

THE FANS

Visitors were an important part of Keiko's life at the Aquarium. An average of 2,500 fans visited him every day at the Oregon Coast Aquarium. A class from Tampa, Florida, that had helped raise funds to rescue Keiko had another fund-raiser so they could come see for themselves how he was doing.

Large windows allowed an underwater view of Keiko's pool. People *oohed* and *aahed* as Keiko cruised by. With his dark eyes—about the size of a cow's—Keiko often paused to watch visitors watch him. Keiko seemed especially interested in small children. In turn, children have sent him hundreds of letters and drawings.

CHANGING VIEWPOINTS

Not long ago, the star treatment of a killer whale would have seemed impossible. For centuries, humans hunted whales. People used whale oil to light their lamps. Ladies used whale-bones in corsets to make their waists seem small. Men hunted whales for sport from boats and planes or used them for target practice. Killer whales were especially feared and hated. Then in the mid-1960s, the public discovered that orcas were not the people-killers they had been thought to be. Instead of fearing orcas, people flocked to marine parks to watch these splashy mammals perform tricks. They saw them as intelligent beings that cooperated with their trainers. Sometimes members of the public were allowed to kiss and hug the whales. And some-times, as in Keiko's case, to swim with them. As Kenneth Balcomb, noted orca researcher explained, orcas developed a kind of "teddy-whale" image that was no more true than that of savage killer.

Today the picture of orcas is once again changing. Thanks to our exposure to captive orcas, people have become curious about the lives of wild whales. Whale watching from boats,

Trainers took turns meeting with Keiko's fans at the Oregon Coast Aquarium during the "Keeper Encounter" to answer the public's questions.

Q. *Is Keiko a fish?*

A. No, Keiko is an air-breathing marine mammal. Other mammals that live in the sea include otters, seals, sea lions, and walruses.

Q. *What has happened to the idea of finding dolphin companions for Keiko?*

A. We've combed the world asking aquariums and others to lend or sell us another whale or a couple of cold-water dolphins, but we've had no luck. That's been a big disappointment of ours.

Q. *Where did Keiko get his name?*

A. He was originally called "Kago." Because Kago sounds too much like a dirty word in Spanish, his name was changed when he began performing in Mexico City. Keiko's name means "Blessed Child" in Japanese.

Q. *How does Keiko make sounds?*

A. By two different means. He makes a clicking noise from his forehead that helps him in echolocation. Sometimes people standing near Keiko can feel him using a "click-train" (a rapid series of clicks) to scan their bodies. Keiko's squeals come from his blowhole. To "speak," Keiko manipulates his nasal sacs and the amount of air passing through it. It's similar to playing with the opening of a balloon as you release the air.

Q. *Does Keiko know what you are trying to do for him?*

A. Who knows exactly what Keiko knows? We feel sure that he knows we care for him a great deal and that he can trust us.

Drawings sent in by Keiko's many fans decorate the trainers' office in Newport, Oregon.

particularly of orcas and gray whales, is becoming increasingly popular. People are beginning to question the right of humans to keep these intelligent creatures in captivity that is so alien from their natural environment. They worry about breaking up the close family bonds of orca societies.

Many people have come to believe that whales, whose brains are three times bigger than ours, are worthy of respect. They have become interested in observing whales and other animals in their own environments.

Keiko has become a kind of ambassador for all whales. Through our experience with Keiko, we have begun asking questions about the right to hold wild animals captive. We have become more aware of the sea, its health, and inhabitants. We acknowledge the beauty and wonder of nature and are inspired to preserve it.

Keiko's sea pen in Klettsvik Bay, Iceland, with the town of Heimay in the background

Ready and Waiting

Why didn't the Foundation choose to keep Keiko safe in his wonderful Aquarium pool for the rest of his life? For one thing, Keiko was alone there. Yes, his trainers swam and played with him every day, but they were slow and clumsy in the water compared to him. They were a lot smaller, too, so he had to be careful around them. Killer whales are usually in touch with their pod. Although his trainers spent many hours each day in Keiko's pool, there were times when no one was there to rub against, to vocalize with, and to play games. And think how many changing sounds ocean living has to offer. At Newport there was the squawking of seagulls and the cries of the new baby otter. But for an animal that learns so much from sound, things must have seemed awfully quiet. By the fall of 1998, Keiko was ready to take to the skies once again.

THE SEA PEN

So how do you keep a whale safe while giving him a chance to enjoy some of the perks of being a wild animal? The Foundation's answer was a sea pen, a kind of halfway house that allows Keiko and his trainers to test the waters.

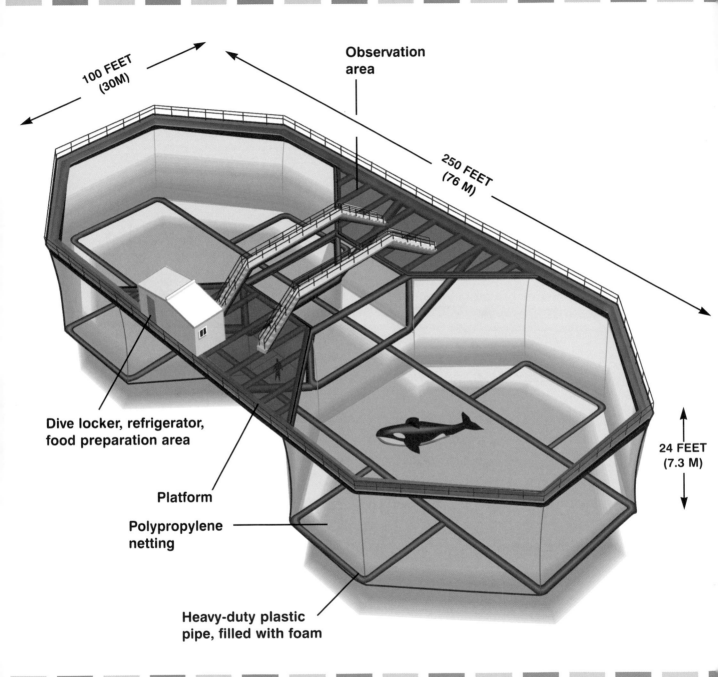

100 FEET
(30M)

Observation area

250 FEET
(76 M)

24 FEET
(7.3 M)

Dive locker, refrigerator, food preparation area

Platform

Polypropylene netting

Heavy-duty plastic pipe, filled with foam

KEIKO'S SEA PEN

COST: $350,000

250 FEET (76 M) LONG

100 FEET (30 M) WIDE

24 FEET (7.3 M) DEEP

VOLUME: 3.2 MILLION GALLONS
(12.1 MILLION L)

TWO TRAINING PLATFORMS
GIVE STAFF MEMBERS EASY
ACCESS TO KEIKO

SMALL STRUCTURE
HOUSES PERSONNEL,
FOOD PREP, DIVING LOCKER,
AND OFFICE

Amusement Park

LOCATION: REINO AVENTURA, MEXICO CITY

DATE: 1985-1995

VOLUME: 500,000 GALLONS (1.89 MILLION L)

Aquarium

LOCATION: OREGON COAST AQUARIUM, NEWPORT

DATE: 1996-1998

VOLUME: 2 MILLION GALLONS (7.57 MILLION L)

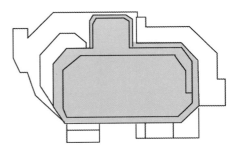

The pen is a safe enclosure for Keiko as he adjusts to life in a natural marine environment for the first time in over nineteen years. It is the largest marine-mammal floating pen ever built. It is wider and deeper than his Aquarium pool, and best of all, it has mesh sides. No more concrete walls to echo back to Keiko. The pen is held fast to the bottom of the bay by huge World War II ship anchors.

THE RIGHT SPOT

In choosing a spot for the pen, the Foundation considered the number of wild whales in the area, the availability of fish, facilities for the staff, and room to provide an educational area for Keiko's visitors. After sampling sediment from the seafloor, testing water quality, studying weather patterns, and researching local and migrating whale populations, the Foundation settled on a small bay in Iceland's Vestmannaeyjar (Westman) Islands

Bay pen

LOCATION: VESTMANNAEYJAR, ICELAND

DATE: SEPT. 1998

VOLUME:
3.2 MILLION GALLONS
(12.1 MILLION L)

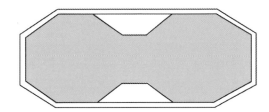

near the town of Heimay. Several killer-whale pods are known to cruise the area at least six months out of the year. Keiko's small bay, a scoop in the side of a larger bay, is nestled among high cliffs. The cliffs provide a chance for visitors to look in on Keiko with spotting scopes or binoculars.

Iceland is a land of ice and fire. In 1973 an eruption on the 5-mile (8-km) -long and 3-mile (5-km)-wide island of Heimay, the largest Westman island, formed a new mountain and increased the island's size by about a third. Unfortunately, half the town was buried in molten lava. Much of the rest was covered in ash. Lava threatened to fill the mouth of the bay. Residents, most of whom depend on the fishing industry, worried that the harbor would be blocked. In a desperate experiment, they poured pour 11.5 million gallons (43.5 million l) of cold water onto the advancing lava. The flow stopped. Today the bay has a narrowed mouth that provides some protection from violent Atlantic storms.

MIXED FEELINGS

Iceland has traditionally been a whaling nation. At first the country was hostile to the idea of hosting the world's most famous whale. Although no commercial whaling is now allowed, sei, fin, sperm, and minke whales were favorite catches until 1989, when Iceland signed an agreement to temporarily stop whaling. Jon Gunnerson, the man who caught Keiko, was disgusted to hear of orca's return. "He should stay put in Oregon!" Gunnerson grumbled.

It is not surprising then, that in the beginning, Iceland wanted nothing to do with the world's most famous whale—a pampered pet that seemed on his way back to freedom. If they should decide to resume whaling, people around the world would think of Keiko and worry about him being caught or killed. There would be protests and bad publicity for Iceland.

Like many nations in the world today, though, Iceland is becoming more environmentally aware. Iceland is said to have the purest water and the cleanest air in the world. Many Icelanders would like to see their country become a leader in environmental issues. They believe hosting Keiko is a great step in that direction. A research facility on Keiko's new island will help the Foundation identify wild pods in the area. And Keiko has made a positive impact on Iceland's tourist industry.

Icelanders are a practical people, not easily impressed by a movie-star whale. But Keiko's homecoming seems to have had some significance for many of them. "You see," one woman related, "we in Iceland have a tradition. When someone is old and ready to die, they return to their place of birth. Keiko was born near here, and now he has returned. Even if he does not survive, it is right that he should come home again."

David Oddsson, Iceland's prime minister, said, "I hope for it [Keiko] to be free at last." Most Icelanders say to Keiko, "*Gott ad vera kommin heim*—It is good to be back home."

We Say 9 Good-bye, You Say Hello

"Good-bye, Keiko." "We love you, Keiko." "Good-bye." It is September 9, 1998. Hundreds of people line the street outside the Oregon Coast Aquarium to wish their neighborhood whale safe travel. A day earlier, nearly 7,000 people crowded into the Aquarium to see Keiko one last time. Once he had been Iceland's whale, then Ontario's, then Mexico City's, and then Portland's. Now Keiko is on his way to his home waters after nineteen years of traveling the entertainment/rehabilitation circuit. The whale whom skeptics said would never again be healthy, would never relearn the skill of catching live fish, would never be welcomed in Iceland, has proved himself again.

Even though Keiko is an international traveler, mailing him back to Iceland is a huge operation—bigger than the trip from Mexico City to Newport. This time Keiko's ten caretakers are moving with him, 4,644 nautical miles (8,600 km) as the C-17 flies. Keiko's flight will last about eight and one-half hours.

THE BIG DAY

Operation Keiko begins like his trip from Mexico City. At 1:00 P.M., Keiko is coaxed into his medical pool, then placed in a sling. The giant crane is back on site, picking up the sling with

KEIKO'S AQUARIUM STATS

	ARRIVAL (January 1996)	DEPARTURE (September 1998)	GOAL
DIVE TIMES (breath holding)	3 minutes	17 minutes, 20 seconds	12 minutes
SPEED	unknown	10 mph (16 kph)	30 mph (48 kph)
WEIGHT	7,720 lbs (3,502 kg)	10,000 lbs (4,536 kg)	10,000 lbs (4,536 kg)
LENGTH	20 feet, 6 inches (6.2 m)	21 feet (6.3 m)	22–27 feet (6.6–8.1 m)
SPYHOPPING HEIGHT	pool not big enough in Mexico City	12–14 feet (3.6–4.2 m)	12–14 feet (3.6–4.2 m)

Keiko inside. Journalists from Germany, Great Britain, Australia, Japan, and Taiwan jostle for a view. Cameras click. British reporter Ben Scotchbrook says, "This story is huge wherever you are in the world."

Keiko makes questioning sounds as he is gently lowered into his crate of water. Handlers notch the sling in place, and Keiko hangs suspended there. The 28-foot (8.5-m) -long crate resembles the borrowed one that brought him to Oregon. This crate is a custom job to accommodate Keiko's three-ton gain. Volunteers form an ice-bucket brigade, dumping the ice into the crate. They want him to be cool and comfortable. Phyllis Bell of the Aquarium says her good-byes.

Keiko's crate is placed on the back of a UPS flatbed truck driven by Ron Kay, the same driver who trucked Keiko to the Aquarium two and a half years before. The truck makes its way down the center of the highway to the Newport airport. The Air Force is not taking any chances with the loading. Keiko and his crate are slid from the truck to a waiting K-9 loader. The loader's bed is then adjusted to the same height as the floor of the plane. The loader crawls up to the tail of the plane, and with the help of a motorized conveyor and several airmen, the crate is winched into the plane's belly.

Because the runway in the Westman Islands is shorter than Newport's, a new kind of plane is needed—a plane that can carry heavy cargo and land on short, narrow runways. A U.S. Air Force cargo plane, the C-17 Globemaster III, proves to be just the thing. It is used by the Air Force to rapidly deploy troops and cargo to remote corners of the world. In fact, it's the *only* aircraft that can carry Keiko to the Westmans. Viewing the operation as a worthwhile effort, the Air Force has agreed to help.

Finally, at 6:25 P.M., the C-17 roars off the runway and on to Iceland. As soon as it reaches its desired altitude, it hooks up with a tanker plane and refuels in midair. A second refueling takes place farther into the trip.

As before, Keiko's veterinarian, Lanny Cornell, is flying in the cargo hold with him. Some of Keiko's trainers are there too. Dressed in wet suits, they are ready to dive into Keiko's container if need be. They rub lotion on his skin to keep it from drying out. Proving once again that Keiko's flight is first-class whale service, the air temperature is kept between 45–50°F (7.2–10°C). A bit chilly for people, but just right for a whale.

THE BIG DAY CONTINUES

It's 10:00 A.M., September 10, Iceland time. Keiko's been in flight for nine hours. Journalists and the townspeople of Heimay wait on a hillside in a stiff wind, straining for sight of the C-17. They mill around speaking in a mix of international languages. They marvel at the bright sun—unusual for this time of year—and at the sparkling sea. A speck finally appears in the sky. It grows

The U.S. Air Force C-17 with Keiko aboard roars to a landing on the Heimay runway.

larger. Although missing a dorsal fin, the object resembles the shape of an oversize orca. It disappears behind a low hill, then reappears over the heads of a group of spectators. Lower and lower it drops until the C-17 is streaking along the runway, its reverse thrusters roaring. Onlookers clap their gloved hands and holler. Photographers scramble to get a better angle.

It's 2:00 P.M. Keiko's trip of 14 hours, from pool to ocean pen, is about to end. Keiko, still in his crate, has been unloaded onto a second UPS truck and driven down the main street of Heimay to the harbor, where a crane hoisted the crate onto a barge that was then tugged out to Klettsvik Bay. Keiko is out of his crate now, dangling in his sling over his new pen. It's been nineteen

Keiko, in his sling, is lifted from his carrier on the barge toward the sea pen in Klettsvik Bay.

Keiko, only a few minutes from his new home.

years since he's been in the North Atlantic. His left pectoral fin dips in the water, yet he doesn't move a muscle. "Is he dead?" someone whispers. "Surely he feels the water. Does he smell it? Do you suppose it smells familiar?"

Slowly, ever so slowly, Keiko is lowered into the sea. Trainers Jeff Foster, Peter Noah, and Brian O'Neal are waiting for him. They spread his sling. Keiko is free to go, but he's not moving. Finally, a flick of his powerful tail flukes and he's out of the sling, cruising the pen and vocalizing excitedly. "Who's out there?" he seems to be saying. He cruises up to Brian, who gives him a reassuring stroke. Trainer Nolan Harvey tosses him a fish. He catches it and gulps it down.

A cheer goes up. "Yeah, Keiko. You've made it! You're the whale!" Journalists, Foundation members, pen construction workers, and keepers all clap their hands. Tears roll down wind-whipped cheeks of men and women. They hug one another. It is a moment to remember. A moment for the history books.

Keeping 10 the Promise

Within three hours of arriving at his new home, Keiko was vocalizing with a pilot whale that had come into his bay. It's the first time since Mexico City that he's been able to "talk" with a fellow cetacean. Imagine the other sounds Keiko must be hearing: The scuttling of crabs on the ocean floor. The cries of wild birds echoing off the cliffs. The movements of the ocean, sometimes lapping and other times crashing against the shore. Fish, large and small. And someday, orcas—pods and super pods of wild orcas, some of which may speak his language.

During his first month in Iceland, Keiko began swimming in patterns like those of wild orcas. He arched his back more and spent much of his time underwater. He's chased and caught live fish that have found their way into his netted pen. Bob Ratliff, executive vice president of the Foundation, said, "He's more active, more aggressive and more curious than in Newport."

It was hoped that the winter of 1999 would find Keiko exchanging greetings with other orcas. But violent storms have kept the usual herring migration from finding their way south. Orcas that follow the herring have not migrated either. Keiko will have to wait a little longer for his first encounter with his own kind.

One might wonder about Keiko being too cold in Iceland after living in Oregon's milder, temperate climate. In fact, chillers kept Keiko's Oregon Coast Aquarium pool slightly colder than his Icelandic bay at the time of his arrival. The Gulf Stream sweeps past the Westman Islands, keeping water temperatures somewhat moderate. As Keiko's first winter progressed, his layer of blubber, the fat just beneath his skin, became thicker, wrapping his body like a warm blanket.

During hurricane-force winds, Keiko has learned to breathe by leaping high above the waves and spray, then diving below the surface again. During the first snowfall of the winter, Keiko spyhopped and caught a few flakes on his tongue. He's also playing with the kelp and other seaweed that grow on the sides of his pen. Just like wild orcas, Keiko drapes it across his dorsal and pectoral fins. It looks like festive streamers as he swims.

The winds may not bother Keiko, but it's another matter for his trainers. The sea pen sometimes rocks violently. All the trainers can do then is wait out the storm in their little bunkhouse on the pen. Air temperature is a challenge for Keiko's trainers, too. They cannot spend much time in the water with Keiko because their face and hands are vulnerable to freezing temperatures the moment they emerge from the water, yet they still give Keiko regular massages and rubdowns with their bare hands. Training time with Keiko is limited during the dark months of the winter. Because Iceland is near the North Pole, there are only three hours of daylight on the shortest day of the year. All this means that Keiko hasn't had a close physical connection to his trainers. That may be good, for it may help him focus on the world below the waters as wild whales do.

When Keiko does work with his trainers, his response time is much faster than at the Aquarium. But the mighty orca is still a

A stronger, livelier
Keiko in Iceland

goof. As Diane Hammond of the Foundation reported in November 1998, "When he is asked to do a speed swim…he does it on his side…with one pectoral fin upraised…. When asked to waggle both pectoral flippers above water, he blows vigorous underwater bubbles from his blowhole instead."

Keiko will continue to live in the sea pen while his survival skills are tested. His keepers will again attach the Keiko Cam to various parts of his body, trying to see just what it is that Keiko does below the waves. Another measuring device, the time device reflector (TDR), is sometimes attached to Keiko by suction cups to tell researchers how fast he swims and how deep he dives. Woods Hole Oceanographic Institution, which began studying Keiko in Newport, continues its study of Keiko's sounds. The Foundation will also be doing photo and vocalization identification of the local orcas during this research phase. And they will begin taking tiny skin samples to see if there is any DNA match to Keiko.

STEP BY STEP

There are plans to string a net across the bay. When his trainers feel Keiko is ready, they will allow him to leave his pen for short periods of time, giving him even more room to exercise. Keepers will keep an eye on him from small boats. After an hour or two, he will be returned to the pen. Will Keiko feel like a kid let out for recess?

If that goes well, someday Keiko will be allowed to swim beyond his own little bay to the broader bay. Then ideally the big, exciting day will come when Keiko the whale tests the mighty Atlantic Ocean for the first time. Even then, Keiko will not be alone. A helicopter will follow his movements. Researchers hope to attach a transmitter to his dorsal fin in a manner similar to ear piercing. The transmitter will be designed to track Keiko for a year. In this way, Keiko will continue to educate us.

THE DREAM

In March 1999, the Free Willy Keiko Foundation and the Jean-Michel Cousteau Institute joined forces to become the Ocean Futures Society, a "voice for the oceans." The Society is dedicated to making a difference in the future quality of human life by restoring the health of the oceans. Its mission is to provide the global community with a forum for exploring issues affecting the oceans, its habitats, and its inhabitants. Jean-Michel Cousteau is president of Ocean Futures. Son of the ocean explorer Jacques Cousteau, Jean-Michel has spent his life exploring the world's oceans aboard the research vessels *Calypso* and *Alcyone*. He continues his work communicating with people of all nations and generations his love and concern for our water planet. Craig McCaw serves as chairman of the board of Ocean Futures.

Jean Michel Cousteau (next to Phyllis Bell, president of the Oregon Coast Aquarium)

Keiko is now Ocean Futures' ambassador, a living symbol of the effect that humans have on marine mammals and the ocean. He continues to raise the world's awareness of the unique role mammals play in the marine environment.

Keiko's family pod may or may not still be intact. Even if it is, we don't know the chances of the pod cruising by Keiko's bay. If it did, would his family recognize or accept him?

Can Keiko survive alone? What are the chances of an unrelated pod striking up a conversation with Keiko? Might they hang around, establish a relationship, and eventually adopt him? No one knows this, either.

We do know that in captivity orcas have remembered former trainers after years of being apart. They also have long memories for routines they've learned. And although they learn new languages from other cetaceans, they do not forget their own. So even after all the years of separation, perhaps…just perhaps…if Keiko's family does exist and if his pod comes calling, they may recognize him. If, miracle of miracles, this happens, it could be eerily similar to the scene in *Free Willy* in which Willy's family calls to him from the bay.

Keiko's supporters love to imagine the magic moment of their reunion. Curious members of his family—his mother and perhaps even his grandmother—will touch their noses to his and brush their sleek bodies against him. Then in a sudden burst of recognition, their rejoicing will begin. Leaping and diving, they'll cavort with one another in sheer joy, their magnificent black-and-white forms flashing in the sun, enjoying the unlimited freedom that nature intended.

Is it only a dream? A movie fantasy? Keiko still has some huge hurdles to overcome. The Ocean Futures Society will not release him from the pen unless they believe he has a high chance of survival. He's got to be healthy. He's got to learn from other orcas where to find food and how to hunt for it. And, perhaps the most important factor—he's going to have to want to be free.

Ocean Futures has a lifetime commitment to Keiko. His trainers will be his pod as long as he wants. Just as he has been since his arrival in Newport, Keiko will be given the opportunity to decide what's next. He will be the one to choose to stay near his human friends or swim away with wild orcas someday.

Two bottlenose dolphins, Bogie and Bacall, were in an experiment similar to Keiko's and had that choice. John Hall, an environmental scientist, observed that during their time in the sea pen the dolphins became more and more interested in their wild counterparts outside their pen and less interested in humans. Finally they chose to join a wild pod.

Millions of people around the world, especially the children, believe that Keiko should have that choice, too. As Craig McCaw, Keiko's real-life guardian angel, says, "The *Free Willy* movie made a promise to the children…a promise that this whale would go free. If Keiko didn't get as close to freedom as we could get him, the promise would be a lie. Keiko's arrival in Iceland proves that dreams can come true. You have the sense that he is home."

GLOSSARY

clan: a temporary joining of pods of related orcas. Also called a *super pod*.

dialect: a form of speech used only by a specific group of orcas.

matrilineal group: a *pod* that is always related to the lead female orca who is often the oldest mother in the *pod*.

offshore whales: also known as the mystery whales, they range far out to sea and are rarely seen.

pod: a family of orcas that always travels together.

resident whales: orcas that frequent a territory near shore. Their main diet is fish.

super pod: see *clan*.

transient whales: orcas that roam over a large area of the ocean, coming and going from the shore. Their main diet is other sea mammals.

SUGGESTED READING

Fromm, Peter J., *Whale Tales*. Friday Harbor, WA: Whale Tales Press, 1995.

Goldner, Kathryn Allen, and Carole Garbury Vogel, *Humphrey, The Wrong Way Whale*. Minneapolis: Dillon Press, 1987.

Gordon, David G., and Chuck Flaherty, *Field Guide to the Orca*. Seattle: Sasquatch Books, 1990.

Graham, Ada and Frank, *Whale Watch: An Audubon Reader*. New York: Delacorte Press, 1980.

Kelsy, Elin, *Finding Out About Whales*. Toronto: Owl Communications, 1998.

McClung, Rober M., *Thor: Last of the Sperm Whales*. Hamden, CT: Linnet Books, 1988.

Morton, Alexandra, *In the Company of Whales*. Custer, WA: Orca Book Publishers, 1993.

Morton, Alexandra, *Switi: A Whale's Story*. Custer, WA: Orca Book Publishers, 1991.

Simon, Seymour, *Whales*. New York: HarperCollins, 1992.

Whittel, Giles, *The Story of Three Whales: A True Adventure*. Milwaukee, WI: Gareth Stevens Children's Books, 1989.

VIDEOS

Free Willy, Free Willy II, Free Willy III, Warner Bros.

The Free Willy Story: Keiko's Journey Home, Discovery Channel, 1996

WEB SITES

Ocean Futures, Keiko's Web site. With the help of the Keiko Cam, "ride" on Keiko's back as he swims and dives in his sea pen. Also get up-to-date reports on what Keiko and his trainers are up to. http://www.oceanfutures.com

The Whale Museum, PO Box 945, Friday Harbor, WA 98250. Orca Adoption Program, 1-800-946-7227. http://whale-museum.org

Cetacean Society International, PO Box 953, Georgetown, CT 06829 http://elfnet1a.elfi.com/csihome.html

Other interesting sites:
http://whales.magna.com.au/faq/index.html (facts about whales)
http://asa.aip.org/sound.html (whale and other interesting sounds)

INDEX